THE

FLORAL DICTIONARY;

OR,

LANGUAGE OF FLOWERS.

BY

ANNA MARIA CAMPBELL.

"A garnered store of precious words
"Hidden in leaves and blushing flowers;
"A language such as the small birds
"Discourse in blossom-bearing bowers."

London:

ROCK BROTHERS, AND PAYNE.

LONDON:
PRINTED BY H. KEMSHEAD,
LOWER KENNINGTON LANE, LAMBETH.

Facsimile reprint
Sphinx House 2016

PREFACE.

FLORAL LANGUAGE, which originated in Eastern climes, where for centuries the loving and the loved have "told in a garland their loves and cares," has of late received much attention throughout Europe. The "Oriental Love-letter," which originally was a simple tulip, implying a declaration of love, or which conveyed by an Ænothera an assignation for evening, has now received such additions, not only from Legends and Poetry, but also from Science, as to be expanded into a volume, and to assume the important title of a FLORAL DICTIONARY.

In the present compilation, the Editor has consulted every authority which was entitled to consideration, from the Romantic Legends which amuse the favorites on the shores of the Bosphorus, to the more sedate but more pleasing records of the accomplished Professor of Botany, Mr. LINDLEY. No historical allusion to a flower has been neglected—no scientific exposition of a flower's qualities has been disregarded; and, in the numerous instances in which conflicting opinions have hitherto disturbed the lovers who "telegraph with flowers," the compiler of the Dictionary has endeavoured to decide so impartially, as to establish his book as an authority, Since precision is at length so nearly attained, that in future

> " token-flowers will tell
> " What words can ne'er express so well,"

it is expected that it will become a matter of re-

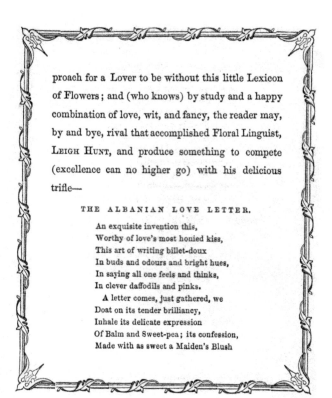

proach for a Lover to be without this little Lexicon
of Flowers; and (who knows) by study and a happy
combination of love, wit, and fancy, the reader may,
by and bye, rival that accomplished Floral Linguist,
LEIGH HUNT, and produce something to compete
(excellence can no higher go) with his delicious
trifle—

THE ALBANIAN LOVE LETTER.

An exquisite invention this,
Worthy of love's most honied kiss,
This art of writing billet-doux
In buds and odours and bright hues,
In saying all one feels and thinks,
In clever daffodils and pinks.
    A letter comes, just gathered, we
Doat on its tender brilliancy,
Inhale its delicate expression
Of Balm and Sweet-pea; its confession,
Made with as sweet a Maiden's Blush

5

As ever morn bedew'd in bush.
And then, when we have kissed its wit
And heart, in water putting it,
To keep its remarks fresh ; go round
Our little eloquent plot of ground,
And with delighted hands compose
Our answer, all of Lily and Rose,
Of Tuberose and Violet,
And little darling Mignonette,
And Gratitude and Polyanthus,
And flowers that say " Felt never Man thus !"

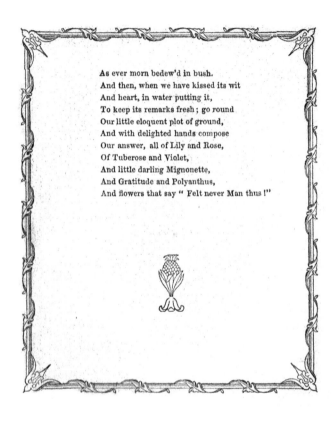

THE FLORAL DICTIONARY;

OR,

LANGUAGE OF FLOWERS.

A

Acacia, *white* .... Friendship, esteem.

Acacia, *rose* .... Taste, elegance.

Acacia, *yellow* .... Jealousy, fear.

Acanthus, *yellow* .... Deceit

Amaranth, *red* .... Everlastingly the same

Amaryllis (day lily) *yellow* ...... Pride, with jealousy

Aconite, *dark blue* .... Misanthropy

Almond Blossom, *pink and white* Early hope, promise

Aloe, out of bloom .... Grief, sorrow

Aloe, in bloom, *white* .... The fulfilment of long hoped-
for joy

Althæa, Garden Mallow, *deep pink* Persuasion

All-heal, or Hercules'-Wound-
wort, *yellow* .... Consolation, I will help you

Anemoné, or Wind Flower, *pale
pink* .... Expectation, coyness, sickness

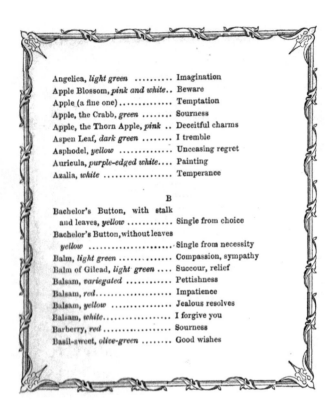

Angelica, *light green* .... Imagination

Apple Blossom, *pink and white* .. Beware

Apple (a fine one) .... Temptation

Apple, the Crabb, *green* .... Sourness

Apple, the Thorn Apple, *pink* .. Deceitful charms

Aspen Leaf, *dark green* .... I tremble

Asphodel, *yellow* .... Unceasing regret

Auricula, *purple-edged white* .... Painting

Azalia, *white* .... Temperance

B

Bachelor's Button, with stalk
and leaves, *yellow* .... Single from choice

Bachelor's Button, without leaves
yellow .... Single from necessity

Balm, *light green* .... Compassion, sympathy

Balm of Gilead, *light green* .... Succour, relief

Balsam, *variegated* .... Pettishness

Balsam, *red* .... Impatience

Balsam, *yellow* .... Jealous resolves

Balsam, *white* .... I forgive you

Barberry, *red* .... Sourness

Basil-sweet, *olive-green* .... Good wishes

Bay Leaf, *dark green* .... I change but in death
Bay Wreath, *dark green* .... Reward of merit
Bee Orchis, (clover) *red* .... Industry
Begonia, *pink, with yellow centre* Flower of the heart, so called
         from the shape of the leaves
Belladonna Lily, *orange and pink* Silence
Bilberry, or Wortleberry, *dark
 purple* .... Treachery
Bird's-foot, *pale yellow* .... Light as a bird
Birdweed, *white* .... Protect me, insinuation
Bitter-sweet, or Nightshade,
 purple, with yellow spot .... Truth
Blackthorn, *white* .... Danger, difficulty
Blue Bell (campanula) *bright blue* Constancy
Blue Bottle (centaury) *light blue* Delicacy
Blue Periwinkle, *light blue* ...... Early friendship
Borage, *light blue* .... Bluntness
Bramble, *white* .... Envy
Branch of Bay, *dark green* ...... A poet's glory
Branch of Thorns, *brown* ...... Punishment
Broom of the Heath, *yellow* .... Meekness
Bugloss, *red* .... Falsehood
Bullrush, *brown* .... Docility

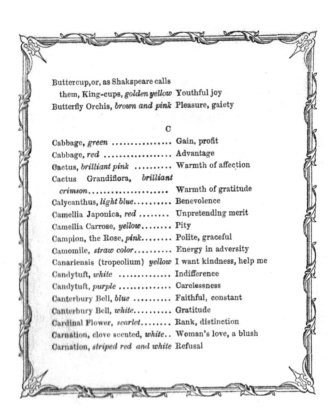

Buttercup, or, as Shakspeare calls
   them, King-cups, *golden yellow* Youthful joy
Butterfly Orchis, *brown and pink* Pleasure, gaiety

C

Cabbage, *green* .... Gain, profit
Cabbage, *red* .... Advantage
Cactus, *brilliant pink* .... Warmth of affection
Cactus Grandiflora, *brilliant
   crimson*..................... Warmth of gratitude
Calycanthus, *light blue*......... Benevolence
Camellia Japonica, *red* .... Unpretending merit
Camellia Carrose, *yellow*....... Pity
Campion, the Rose, *pink*........ Polite, graceful
Camomile, *straw color*.......... Energy in adversity
Canariensis (tropeolium) *yellow* I want kindness, help me
Candytuft, *white* .... Indifference
Candytuft, *purple* .... Carelessness
Canterbury Bell, *blue* .... Faithful, constant
Canterbury Bell, *white*......... Gratitude
Cardinal Flower, *scarlet*....... Rank, distinction
Carnation, clove scented, *white*.. Woman's love, a blush
Carnation, *striped red and white* Refusal

Carnation, *yellow* .... Dislike
Cassia, dwarf, *yellow* .... Abundance
Catch Fly, *scarlet* .... Deception
Cedar Leaf (fennel) *green* ...... I live only for you
Celadine, *yellow green*.......... Happiness to come
Chickweed, *white* .... A day appointment, if the day
                                 is fine, as the flower closes
                                 when it rains, and at night
China Aster (single) *purple* .... Disappointment
China Aster, *variegated* .... Variety
China Aster (double) *purple* .... I think with you
China Aster (single) *pink or white* I will think of it
China, or Indian Pink, *red*...... Dislike, aversion
China, or Monthly Rose, *a deli-*
  cate pink .... Beauty ever new
Chrysanthemum, *rose colored* .. Cheerful, though unfortunate
Chrysanthemum, *red* .... I love
Chrysanthemum, *white* .... Truth
Chrysanthemum, *yellow* .... Slighted love
Cinquefoil (clover grass) *white* .. Beloved daughter
Citron, *green* .... Beauty with ill humour
Clarkia (Pulchella) *pink & white* Refinement, elegance
Clary, or Cleary, *purple top* .... Welcome news

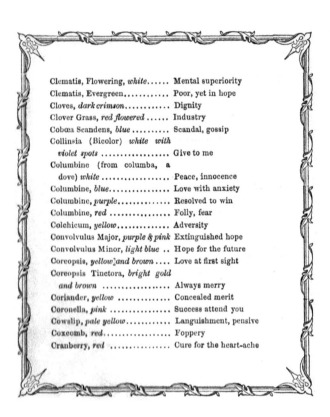

Clematis, Flowering, *white*...... Mental superiority

Clematis, Evergreen........... Poor, yet in hope

Cloves, *dark crimson*........... Dignity

Clover Grass, *red flowered* ..... Industry

Cobœa Scandens, *blue* .... Scandal, gossip

Collinsia (Bicolor) *white with violet spots* .... Give to me

Columbine (from columba, a dove) *white* .... Peace, innocence

Columbine, *blue*............... Love with anxiety

Columbine, *purple*............. Resolved to win

Columbine, *red* .... Folly, fear

Colchicum, *yellow*............. Adversity

Convolvulus Major, *purple & pink* Extinguished hope

Convolvulus Minor, *light blue* .. Hope for the future

Coreopsis, *yellow and brown* .... Love at first sight

Coreopsis Tinctora, *bright gold and brown* .... Always merry

Coriander, *yellow* .... Concealed merit

Coronella, *pink* .... Success attend you

Cowslip, *pale yellow*........... Languishment, pensive

Coxcomb, *red*.................. Foppery

Cranberry, *red* .... Cure for the heart-ache

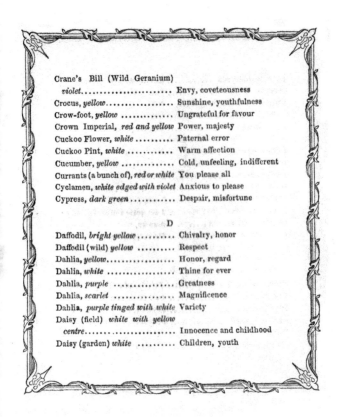

Crane's Bill (Wild Geranium)
violet...................... Envy, coveteousness
Crocus, *yellow*.................. Sunshine, youthfulness
Crow-foot, *yellow* .... Ungrateful for favour
Crown Imperial, *red and yellow* Power, majesty
Cuckoo Flower, *white* .... Paternal error
Cuckoo Pint, *white* .... Warm affection
Cucumber, *yellow* .... Cold, unfeeling, indifferent
Currants (a bunch of), *red or white* You please all
Cyclamen, *white edged with violet* Anxious to please
Cypress, *dark green* .... Despair, misfortune

D

Daffodil, *bright yellow* .... Chivalry, honor
Daffodil (wild) *yellow* .... Respect
Dahlia, *yellow*.................. Honor, regard
Dahlia, *white* .... Thine for ever
Dahlia, *purple* .... Greatness
Dahlia, *scarlet* .... Magnificence
Dahlia, *purple tinged with white* Variety
Daisy (field) *white with yellow
centre*...................... Innocence and childhood
Daisy (garden) *white* .... Children, youth

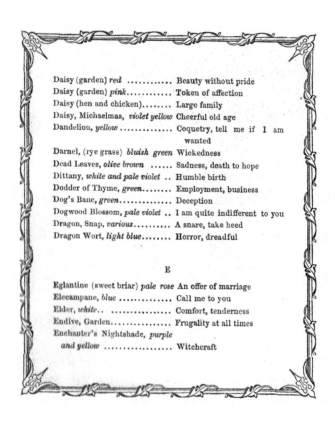

Daisy (garden) *red* .... Beauty without pride
Daisy (garden) *pink*............ Token of affection
Daisy (hen and chicken)........ Large family
Daisy, Michaelmas, *violet yellow* Cheerful old age
Dandelion, *yellow* .... Coquetry, tell me if I am
                                      wanted
Darnel, (rye grass) *bluish green* Wickedness
Dead Leaves, *olive brown* ...... Sadness, death to hope
Dittany, *white and pale violet* .. Humble birth
Dodder of Thyme, *green*........ Employment, business
Dog's Bane, *green*............. Deception
Dogwood Blossom, *pale violet* .. I am quite indifferent to you
Dragon, Snap, *various*.......... A snare, take heed
Dragon Wort, *light blue*........ Horror, dreadful

E

Eglantine (sweet briar) *pale rose* An offer of marriage
Elecampane, *blue* .... Call me to you
Elder, *white*.. .... Comfort, tenderness
Endive, Garden................ Frugality at all times
Enchanter's Nightshade, *purple
  and yellow* .... Witchcraft

14

Eringo (Sea Holly) *blue* .... News from sea, or afar
Evening Primrose, *yellow* ...... Sighs, an appointment for the evening
Everlasting Pea, *pink* .... Continued pleasure
Everlasting Flower, *yellow* ...... Never forget, immortal
Eye Bright, or Wake Robin, *scarlet* Joyful tidings

F

Fair Maid of France (the White Bachelor's Button, applicable to ladies only) with leaves, *white* .... Single from choice
Fair Maid of France, without leaves, *white* .... Single from necessity
Fennel, *yellow* .... Strength of mind
Fig, *green* .... I do not care for you
Fig, Ripe, *purple green* .... Argument
Filbert, *green and bright brown* Reconciliation
Fir Tree, *green* .... Prosperity, elevation
Flax, *blue* .... Domestic industry
Flax-leaved Golden Locks, *yellow* Laziness, idle
Flos Aëris, *blue and pale pink* .. Lightness
Fly Orchis, *blue* .... Mistake, error

Forget-me-not, *cerulean blue*.... Forget me not
Fox Glove, *white or pink*........ Falsehood
French Honeysuckle, *red* ...... Rustic beauty
French Marygold, *gold colour* .. Doubt, jealousy
French Willow, *pink*............ Courage, bravery
Fuschia, *crimson and purple* .... Accepted love

G

Geranium, *scarlet*.............. Home, a place of rest
Geranium (ivy) *violet* .... I engage you for the next
dance
Geranium (oak) *pink* .... Lady deign to smile
Geranium (silver-leaved) *pink* .. Come back again
Geranium (nutmeg) *pink*....... An expected meeting
Geranium (large) *pink*.......... I prefer you
Gilly Flower, *red* .... Unfading beauty
Globe-Amaranth, *purple*....... True to eternity
Goats' Rue, *violet* .... Reason
Golden Rod, *deep yellow* ...... Encouragement
Gooseberry, *red or green*....... Anticipation
Gorse, *yellow* .... Displeasure
Gourd, *yellow*................. Bulk
Grape, *purple*................. Rural joy, gladness

Grass, *green* .... Submission, utility
Ground-Ivy, *purple* .... Domestic comfort
Guelder Rose, *white*........... Age with friendship

H

Hare Bell, *blue* .... Retirement
Hawkweed, *pink* .... Clear sightedness
Hawkweed, *yellow* .... Support me or I fall
Hawthorn, *white* .... Hope
Hawthorn, *pink*............... Rural beauty
Heartsease (pansy) *purple yellow* Thoughts
Heartsease (wild) *purple yellow* A kiss at the garden gate
Heartsease, *purple* .... I think on you
Heartsease, *purple edged with*
   yellow .... Heartsease, happiness
Heath, *white or pink*........... Solitude
Heath, *purple* .... Liberty
Heliotrope, Cherry - pie Plant,
   violet .... Devoted attachment
Hellebore (Christmas Rose) *white* Calumny, inconstancy
Helmet Flower, or Monk's-hood,
   purple .... Chivalry, knighthood
Hemlock, *purple* .... You will cause my death

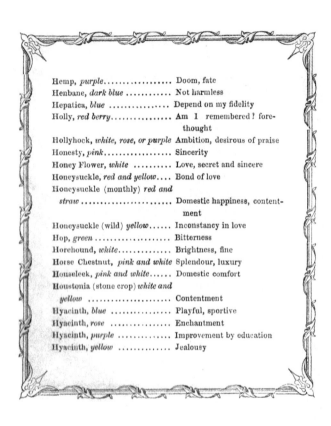

Hemp, *purple*.................. Doom, fate

Henbane, *dark blue* .... Not harmless

Hepatica, *blue* .... Depend on my fidelity

Holly, *red berry*.............. Am I remembered? fore-
thought

Hollyhock, *white, rose, or purple* Ambition, desirous of praise

Honesty, *pink*................... Sincerity

Honey Flower, *white* .... Love, secret and sincere

Honeysuckle, *red and yellow*.... Bond of love

Honeysuckle (monthly) *red and
straw* .... Domestic happiness, contentment

Honeysuckle (wild) *yellow*...... Inconstancy in love

Hop, *green* .... Bitterness

Horehound, *white*.............. Brightness, fine

Horse Chestnut, *pink and white* Splendour, luxury

Houseleek, *pink and white*..... Domestic comfort

Houstonia (stone crop) *white and
yellow* .... Contentment

Hyacinth, *blue* .... Playful, sportive

Hyacinth, *rose* .... Enchantment

Hyacinth, *purple* .... Improvement by education

Hyacinth, *yellow* .... Jealousy

Hydrangea, *pink or violet* ...... Ostentation, falsehood
Hysop, *white* .... Purity, cleanliness

I

Ice Plant, *pale pink* .... I refuse you, winter
Indian or Sweet Scabious, *dark violet* .... I have lost all
Indian Cress, *yellow* .... A trophy of victory
Indian Pink, *dark pink* .... Always lovely
Iris, *blue-white* .... I have a message to you
Iris, *yellow* .... I am jealous
Iris (pencilled) *blue-white* ...... Hope
Ivy, *green* .... Attachment, I cling to you

J

Japan Rose, *red* .... Beauty is all your attraction
Jasmine, *white* .... Amiable and sincere
Jasmine, *yellow* .... Elegance and grace
Jasmine Cape, *blue* .... Transport of joy
Jonquil, *yellow* .... Desire, I desire a return of love
Juniper, *yellow* .... Help or protection

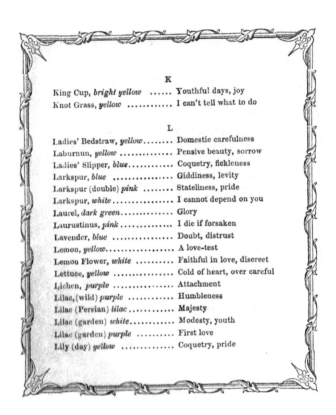

K

King Cup, *bright yellow* ...... Youthful days, joy
Knot Grass, *yellow* .... I can't tell what to do

L

Ladies' Bedstraw, *yellow* .... Domestic carefulness
Laburnum, *yellow* .... Pensive beauty, sorrow
Ladies' Slipper, *blue* .... Coquetry, fickleness
Larkspur, *blue* .... Giddiness, levity
Larkspur (double) *pink* .... Stateliness, pride
Larkspur, *white* .... I cannot depend on you
Laurel, *dark green* .... Glory
Laurustinus, *pink* .... I die if forsaken
Lavender, *blue* .... Doubt, distrust
Lemon, *yellow* .... A love-test
Lemon Flower, *white* .... Faithful in love, discreet
Lettuce, *yellow* .... Cold of heart, over careful
Lichen, *purple* .... Attachment
Lilac, (wild) *purple* .... Humbleness
Lilac (Persian) *lilac* .... Majesty
Lilac (garden) *white* .... Modesty, youth
Lilac (garden) *purple* .... First love
Lily (day) *yellow* .... Coquetry, pride

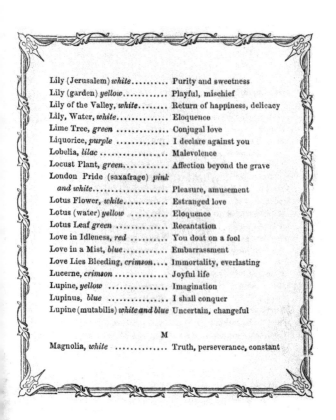

Lily (Jerusalem) *white*......... Purity and sweetness
Lily (garden) *yellow*........... Playful, mischief
Lily of the Valley, *white*....... Return of happiness, delicacy
Lily, Water, *white*............. Eloquence
Lime Tree, *green* .... Conjugal love
Liquorice, *purple* .... I declare against you
Lobelia, *lilac* .... Malevolence
Locust Plant, *green*........... Affection beyond the grave
London Pride (saxafrage) *pink and white*................... Pleasure, amusement
Lotus Flower, *white*........... Estranged love
Lotus (water) *yellow* .... Eloquence
Lotus Leaf *green* .... Recantation
Love in Idleness, *red* .... You doat on a fool
Love in a Mist, *blue*........... Embarrassment
Love Lies Bleeding, *crimson*.... Immortality, everlasting
Lucerne, *crimson* .... Joyful life
Lupine, *yellow* .... Imagination
Lupinus, *blue* .... I shall conquer
Lupine (mutabilis) *white and blue* Uncertain, changeful

M

Magnolia, *white* .... Truth, perseverance, constant

21

Maiden Hair, *white* .... Secret, discreet

Maid Wort, *white* .... Single

Mallow, *white* .... Mildness

Mallow (marsh) *yellow* .... Benevolent, useful

Mallow (garden) *pink* .... Live for me, persuasion

Malope (grandiflora) *crimson* .... Consumed by love

Marigold, *bright yellow* .... The French call it *sans souci*, (devoid of care) Shakspeare calls it " A flower of mature age," and signifies welcome

Marjoram, *violet* .... Blushes, welcome

Marvel of Peru, *red or yellow* .... Evening, timidity

Meadow Saffron, *yellow* .... My best days are over

Meadow Lychnis, *pink* .... Vivacity, wit

Meadow sweet, *white* .... Useless, though pretty

Mezereon, *red* .... I wish to please

Mignonette, *green and speckled with red* .... Sweetness, your virtues surpass your beauty

Michaelmas Daisy, *white and red* Late blossoms

Milfoil (yarrow) *yellow* .... Discord, war

Milfoil (garden yarrow) *dark pink* I shall quarrel

Milk Vetch, *white* .... Your presence softens my pain

22

Mimosa (sensitive plant) *pale yel-
low* .... Sensitiveness, touch me not
Mint, *green* .... Virtue
Miseltoe of the Oak, *white* ...... Difficulties surmounted, a kiss
Moon Wort, *green and white* .... Forgetfulness
Moss, *green* .... Motherly love, retirement
Mouse-car, *blue* .... Ingenuous simplicity
Mountain Laurel, *pale pink* .... Excellent, exalted
Mug-wort, *light blue and pink* .. Happiness
Mulberry, *brown purple* .... Wisdom
Mullein, *blueish red* .... Good nature
Mushroom, *brownish white* .... Suspicion
Mustard Seed, *yellow* .... Want of affection
Myrrh, *green* .... Glad, joyful
Myrtle, *white* .... Friendship and love

N

Narcissus, *white* .... You admire yourself
Nasturtium, *yellow* .... Patriotism
Nasturtium, *scarlet* .... Splendour
Nasturtium (sanguinary) *dark red* Trophy of war
Nemophilla, *cerulean blue* ...... Sincere and unpresuming love
Nettle, dead, *white* .... Harmless

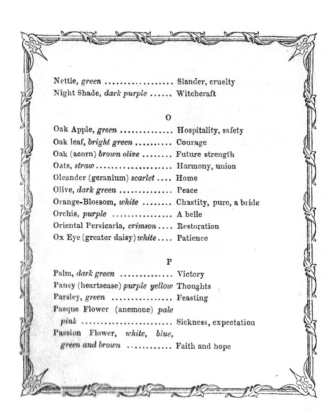

Nettle, *green* .... Slander, cruelty
Night Shade, *dark purple* ...... Witchcraft

O

Oak Apple, *green* .... Hospitality, safety
Oak leaf, *bright green* .... Courage
Oak (acorn) *brown olive* .... Future strength
Oats, *straw* .... Harmony, union
Oleander (geranium) *scarlet* .... Home
Olive, *dark green* .... Peace
Orange-Blossom, *white* .... Chastity, pure, a bride
Orchis, *purple* .... A belle
Oriental Persicaria, *crimson* .... Restoration
Ox Eye (greater daisy) *white* .... Patience

P

Palm, *dark green* .... Victory
Pansy (heartsease) *purple yellow* Thoughts
Parsley, *green* .... Feasting
Pasque Flower (anemone) *pale
pink* .... Sickness, expectation
Passion Flower, *white, blue,
green and brown* .... Faith and hope

Pea (sweet) *white or pink*	Respect and love
Pea (sweet) *purple or dark pink*	Respect and friendship
Pea Everlasting, *pink*	Continued pleasure
Peach Blossom, *pale pink*	I am your captive
Penny Royal, *dark green*	Flee away
Peony, *crimson*	Anger, gaudiness
Peony, *white*	Blushes, timidity
Periwinkle, *blue*	Pleasure of memory
Periwinkle, *red*	Remember early friendship
Periwinkle, *white*	Remember our childhood
Peruvian Heliotrope, *violet*	Devoted attachment
Pheasant's Eye, *scarlet*	Sorrow, remembrance
Phlox, *white*	Unanimity
Phlox, *blue*	I agree to your wish
Pimpernel (chickweed) *white*	An appointment
Pimpernel, *scarlet*	Foretells tears
Pine Apple, *yellow*	Perfection
Pink, *white*	Fair and pleasing
Pink, *white, edged with pink*	An offering
Pink, *carnation*	Woman's love
Pink (double) *red*	Ardent love
Pink (Indian) *dark pink*	Always lovely
Pleurisy Root, *brown*	Cure for the heartache

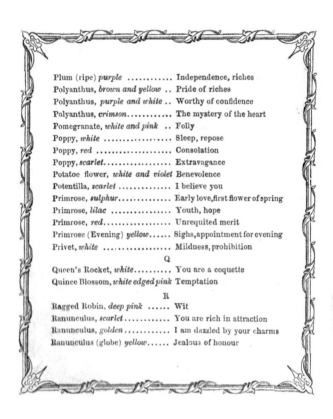

Plum (ripe) *purple* .... Independence, riches
Polyanthus, *brown and yellow* .. Pride of riches
Polyanthus, *purple and white* .. Worthy of confidence
Polyanthus, *crimson*............ The mystery of the heart
Pomegranate, *white and pink* .. Folly
Poppy, *white* .... Sleep, repose
Poppy, *red* .... Consolation
Poppy, *scarlet*................. Extravagance
Potatoe flower, *white and violet* Benevolence
Potentilla, *scarlet* .... I believe you
Primrose, *sulphur*............. Early love, first flower of spring
Primrose, *lilac* .... Youth, hope
Primrose, *red*................. Unrequited merit
Primrose (Evening) *yellow*...... Sighs, appointment for evening
Privet, *white* .... Mildness, prohibition

Q

Queen's Rocket, *white*......... You are a coquette
Quince Blossom, *white edged pink* Temptation

R

Ragged Robin, *deep pink* ...... Wit
Ranunculus, *scarlet* .... You are rich in attraction
Ranunculus, *golden* .... I am dazzled by your charms
Ranunculus (globe) *yellow*...... Jealous of honour

Ranunculus (wild) *yellow* ...... Youthful joy
Ranunculus, *variegated* .... Aspiring
Raspberry, *red* .... Remorse
Reed (common) *brown* .... Desirous to please
Reed (split) *brown* .... Indiscretion
Reeds, *brown* .... Harmony, music
Rhubarb, *light straw* .... Advice
Rose (Full Blown) *red* .... Happy love, beauty
Rose (Multiflora China) *red* .... Beauty with dignity
Rose Musk (cluster of) *red* .... You are charming
Rose (cabbage) *red* .... Ambassador of love
Rose (maiden's blush) *pale pink* Will you love me
Rose (monthly) *pink* .... Thy smile I hope for
Rose (damask) *red* .... Successful love
Rose, Moss (full blown) *pink* .... Superior merit
Rose, Moss (bud) *pink* .... Confession of love
Rose (full blown) *white* .... I am worthy of you
Rose (faded) *any color* .... Hope told a flattering tale
Rose (faded) *yellow* .... Decrease of affection
Rose (variegated) *pink and white* War or peace
Rose (York and Lancaster).... United in peace
Rose (full blown) over two buds Paternal approbation
Rosebud, *red* .... Declaration of love
Rosebud, *white* .... A heart ignorant of love

Rosebud (maiden's blush) *white* If you love me you'll find me
Rosemary, *green* .... Remembrance, welcome
Rue, *dark green* .... Herb of grace
Rush, *green* .... Docility

S.

Saffron, *golden yellow* .... Hymen, matrimony
Sage, *dark green* .... Wisdom, domestic virtue
Scabious (starry) *dark purple* .. I have lost all
Scabious (sweet) *dark purple* .. Widowhood
Scabious (corn flower) *blue* .... Plenty
Scarlet Lychnis, *scarlet* .... Eyes bright as the sun
Sensitive Plant, *green* .... Susceptibility
Shamrock, *green* .... Light heartedness
Snake Tongue, *olive green* ...... Slander
Snap Dragon, *various* .... A snare, take heed
Snow Drop, *white* .... Confidence in the future
Sorrel (garden) *red* .... Parental affection
Sorrel (wild) *green* .... Ill-timed raillery
Southernwood, *green* .... An old man, jesting
Speedwell, *blue* .... Faithful, true, celerity
Spider Wort, *blue with yellow* .. Esteem, but not love
St. John's Wort, Satin Flower, Superstition, truth
Star of Bethlehem, *yellow* ...... Guidance, reconciliation

Star Wort, Michaelmas Daisy, *yel.* Late blossoms
Star Wort, *violet* .... Welcome to strangers
Star Wort, *red and blue* .... Cheerfulness in old age
Stock (Gilly Flower) *red* .... Lasting beauty
Stock, *purple* .... Bounty
Strawberry, *scarlet* .... Perfection
Strawberry Leaf, *green* .... Love and esteem
Sunflower (dwarf) *yellow* .... Adoration, I turn to thee
Sunflower (tall) *yellow* .... Constancy, pride
Sweet Briar, *pink* .... Offer of marriage
Sweet Peas (a bunch) *all colors* Dependence
Sweet Sultan, *yellow* .... Gallantry
Sweet William, *variegated* ...... Gallantry
Sweet William, *dark red* .... Maturity
Sweet William (double) *white* .. Finesse
Syringa, *primrose* .... Disappointment

T

Tansy, *yellow* .... Resistance
Ten Weeks' Stock, *red* .... Promptitude
Thistle, *blue* .... Austerity
Thistle (Scotch) *purple* .... Retaliation
Thrift, *crimson* .... Mutual sympathy
True Love, *red* .... True love

Throat Wort, *pale blue* .... Neglected beauty
Thyme, *violet* .... Activity
Trefoil, *green* .... Unity
Traveller's Joy, *white* .... Safety
Tuber-rose, *pink* .... The further the dearer
Tulip Tree, *white* .... Fame
Tulip, *red* .... Declaration of love
Tulip (variegated) *gold and brown* Beautiful eyes
Tulip, *yellow* .... Hopeless love
Turnip, *yellow* .... Charity

V

Valerian, *scarlet* .... Accommodate to reconcile
Venus's Looking Glass, *pink*.... Flattery
Verbena, *rose* .... Sensibility
Verbena, *scarlet*............... Brilliant talents
Verbena, *white* .... Modesty, content
Vernal Grass, *green*............ Poor, but happy
Veronica, *blue, white, or pink* .. Patience
Violet, *purple and white* .... Perseverance, modesty
Vine, *purple* .... Rural joy
Vine Leaf, *green* .... Friendship
Vine-Wreath with Grapes, *purple* Intoxication

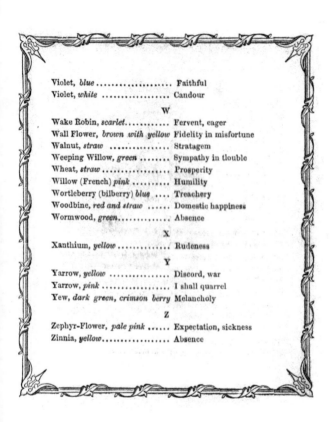

Violet, *blue* .... Faithful
Violet, *white* .... Candour

W

Wake Robin, *scarlet*........... Fervent, eager
Wall Flower, *brown with yellow* Fidelity in misfortune
Walnut, *straw* .... Stratagem
Weeping Willow, *green* .... Sympathy in trouble
Wheat, *straw* .... Prosperity
Willow (French) *pink* .... Humility
Wortleberry (bilberry) *blue* .... Treachery
Woodbine, *red and straw* ...... Domestic happiness
Wormwood, *green*............. Absence

X

Xanthium, *yellow* .... Rudeness

Y

Yarrow, *yellow* .... Discord, war
Yarrow, *pink* .... I shall quarrel
Yew, *dark green, crimson berry* Melancholy

Z

Zephyr-Flower, *pale pink* ...... Expectation, sickness
Zinnia, *yellow*................. Absence

Groups & Messages.

A Rose ....
A Pink .... } Love offering heartsease
A Heartsease ....

A Rose ....
Sweet-Briar .... } Love offers marriage, a home
Geranium ....   and domestic comfort
Ground-Ivy ....

St. John's-Wort .... } Truth.   I only live for you.
A Leaf of Fennel..........

Garden Yarrow .... } I shall quarrel. I am jealous
The Yellow Flag...........

Scotch Thistle ....
Snap Dragon............... } Retalliation, a snare, beware
Apple-Blossom.............

Snow Drop .... } Confidence in future love
Rose ....

Flax ....
Scarlet Potentilla .... } I feel much obliged, I believe
Narcissus ....   you admire yourself

Iris, *blue*............... } I have a message to you, I do
A Fig ....   not care for you

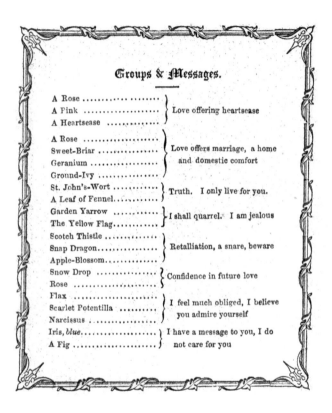

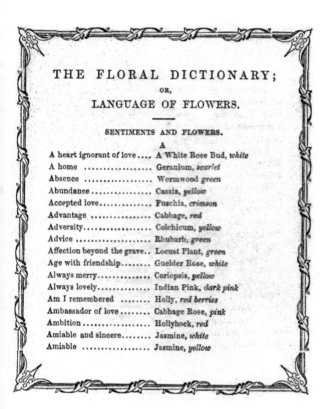

THE FLORAL DICTIONARY;

OR,

LANGUAGE OF FLOWERS.

SENTIMENTS AND FLOWERS.

A

A heart ignorant of love	A White Rose Bud, *white*
A home	Geranium, *scarlet*
Absence	Wormwood *green*
Abundance	Cassia, *yellow*
Accepted love..............	Fuschia, *crimson*
Advantage	Cabbage, *red*
Adversity.................	Colchicum, *yellow*
Advice	Rhubarb, *green*
Affection beyond the grave..	Locust Plant, *green*
Age with friendship........	Guelder Rose, *white*
Always merry..............	Coriopsis, *yellow*
Always lovely..............	Indian Pink, *dark pink*
Am I remembered	Holly, *red berries*
Ambassador of love	Cabbage Rose, *pink*
Ambition	Hollyhock, *red*
Amiable and sincere........	Jasmine, *white*
Amiable	Jasmine, *yellow*

An appointment for a fine day .... Chickweed
An appointment for evening .... Evening Primrose
An expected meeting ...... Nutmeg Geranium, *pink*
Anger .... Peony, *crimson*
Anticipation .... Gooseberry, *green or ripe*
Anxious to please .... Cyclamen, *white edged*
Ardent love............... Double Pink, *red*
Argument .... A Ripe Fig, *purple*
Aspiring .... Ranunculus, *variegated*
Attachment............... Ivy, *green*

B

Beauty ever new .... China Rose, *delicate pink*
Beauty without pride ...... Daisy, *red*
Beauty with ill humour .... Citron, *green*
Beauty with dignity........ China Rose Multiflora, *red*
Beauty is all your attraction Japan Rose (scentless)
Beautiful eyes .... Tulip, *gold and brown*
Benevolence .... Calycanthus, or Potatoe Blossom
Benevolent .... Marsh Mallow, *yellow*
Beware.................... Apple Blossom, *pink and white*
Blushes .... Tulip, or Marjoram
Bond of love .... Honeysuckle, *red*
Brightness .... Horehound, *white*

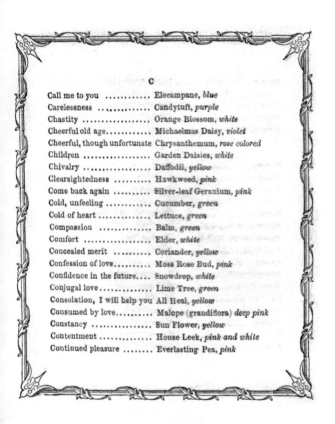

C

Call me to you	Elecampane, *blue*
Carelessness	Candytuft, *purple*
Chastity	Orange Blossom, *white*
Cheerful old age	Michaelmas Daisy, *violet*
Cheerful, though unfortunate	Chrysanthemum, *rose colored*
Children	Garden Daisies, *white*
Chivalry	Daffodil, *yellow*
Clearsightedness	Hawkweed, *pink*
Come back again	Silver-leaf Geranium, *pink*
Cold, unfeeling	Cucumber, *green*
Cold of heart	Lettuce, *green*
Compassion	Balm, *green*
Comfort	Elder, *white*
Concealed merit	Coriander, *yellow*
Confession of love	Moss Rose Bud, *pink*
Confidence in the future	Snowdrop, *white*
Conjugal love	Lime Tree, *green*
Consolation, I will help you	All Heal, *yellow*
Consumed by love	Malope (grandiflora) *deep pink*
Constancy	Sun Flower, *yellow*
Contentment	House Leek, *pink and white*
Continued pleasure	Everlasting Pea, *pink*

Coquetry, fickleness....... Lady's Slipper, *blue*
Coquetry, pride........... Day Lily, *yellow*
Coquetry, am I wanted .... Dandelion, *yellow*
Courage .... Oak Leaf, or French Willow
Cure for the heartache .... Cranberry, *red*

D

Danger................... Blackthorn, *white*
Deception .... Catch Fly, *scarlet*
Declaration of love .... Rosebud, or Tulip, *red*
Decrease of affection ...... Rose, *yellow*
Delicacy .... Blue Bottle, *light blue*
Delicate pleasure .... Sweet Pea, *pink*
Depend on my fidelity...... Hepatica, *blue*
Desire .... Jonquil, *yellow*
Despair .... Cypress, *dark green*
Devoted attachment........ Heliotrope, *violet*
Disappointment........... Syringa, *primrose*
Dislike................... Carnation, or Indian Pink
Displeasure............... Gorse, *yellow*
Discord .... Yarrow, *yellow*
Distinction .... Cardinal Flower, *crimson*
Domestic comfort......... Houseleek, *pink and white*

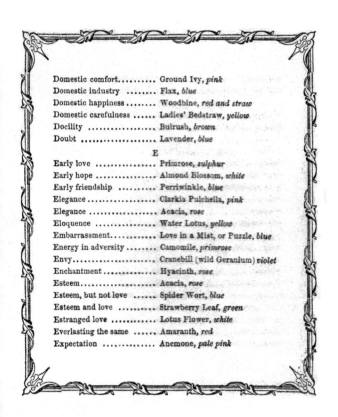

Domestic comfort.......... Ground Ivy, *pink*
Domestic industry .... Flax, *blue*
Domestic happiness .... Woodbine, *red and straw*
Domestic carefulness ...... Ladies' Bedstraw, *yellow*
Docility .... Bulrush, *brown*
Doubt .... Lavender, *blue*

E

Early love .... Primrose, *sulphur*
Early hope .... Almond Blossom, *white*
Early friendship .... Perriwinkle, *blue*
Elegance .... Clarkia Pulchella, *pink*
Elegance .... Acacia, *rose*
Eloquence .... Water Lotus, *yellow*
Embarrassment............. Love in a Mist, or Puzzle, *blue*
Energy in adversity .... Camomile, *primrose*
Envy...................... Cranebill (wild Geranium) *violet*
Enchantment .... Hyacinth, *rose*
Esteem..................... Acacia, *rose*
Esteem, but not love ...... Spider Wort, *blue*
Esteem and love .... Strawberry Leaf, *green*
Estranged love .... Lotus Flower, *white*
Everlasting the same ...... Amaranth, *red*
Expectation .... Anemone, *pale pink*

37

Extinguished hope .... Convolvulus Major, *purple, pink*
Eyes bright as the sun...... Lychnis, *scarlet*

F

Falsehood .... Bugloss, *blue*
Fame...................... Tulip Tree, *white*
Faithful .... Canterbury Bell, *blue*
Faithful .... Violet, *blue*
Faithful in love .... Lemon Flower, *white*
Faith and Hope .... Passion Flower, *blue, white*
Fair and Pleasing.......... A Garden Pink, *white*
Fear .... Acacia, *yellow*
Fear .... Columbine, *red*
First flower of spring ..... Primrose, *sulphur*
First love................. Lilac, *purple*
Flower of the heart .... Begonia, *pink, yellow centre*
Flattery .... Venus's Looking Glass, *pink*
Foppery .... Coxcomb, *crimson*
Folly .... Columbine, *red*
Forget me–not .... Forget-me-not, *cerulean blue*
Friendship .... Acacia, *rose*
Friendship and love........ Myrtle, *green*
Friendship .... A Vine Leaf, *green*
Fulfilment of hoped for joy.. Aloe, *pink, white*

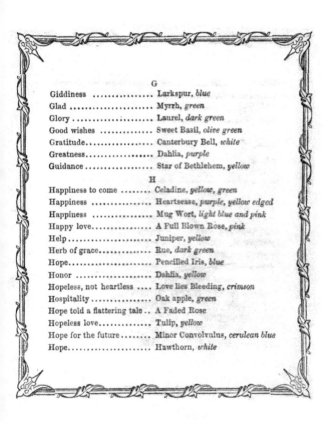

G

Giddiness	Larkspur, *blue*
Glad	Myrrh, *green*
Glory	Laurel, *dark green*
Good wishes	Sweet Basil, *olive green*
Gratitude	Canterbury Bell, *white*
Greatness	Dahlia, *purple*
Guidance	Star of Bethlehem, *yellow*

H

Happiness to come	Celadine, *yellow, green*
Happiness	Heartsease, *purple, yellow edged*
Happiness	Mug Wort, *light blue and pink*
Happy love	A Full Blown Rose, *pink*
Help	Juniper, *yellow*
Herb of grace	Rue, *dark green*
Hope	Pencilled Iris, *blue*
Honor	Dahlia, *yellow*
Hopeless, not heartless	Love lies Bleeding, *crimson*
Hospitality	Oak apple, *green*
Hope told a flattering tale	A Faded Rose
Hopeless love	Tulip, *yellow*
Hope for the future	Minor Convolvulus, *cerulean blue*
Hope	Hawthorn, *white*

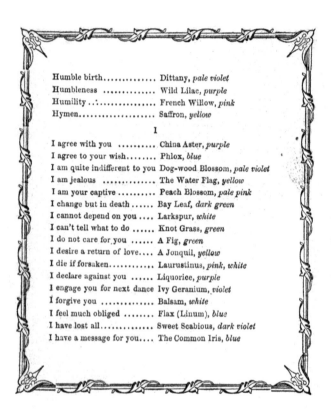

Humble birth............. Dittany, *pale violet*
Humbleness .... Wild Lilac, *purple*
Humility .... French Willow, *pink*
Hymen................... Saffron, *yellow*

I

I agree with you .... China Aster, *purple*
I agree to your wish........ Phlox, *blue*
I am quite indifferent to you Dog-wood Blossom, *pale violet*
I am jealous .... The Water Flag, *yellow*
I am your captive .... Peach Blossom, *pale pink*
I change but in death ...... Bay Leaf, *dark green*
I cannot depend on you .... Larkspur, *white*
I can't tell what to do ...... Knot Grass, *green*
I do not care for you ...... A Fig, *green*
I desire a return of love .... A Jonquil, *yellow*
I die if forsaken............ Laurustinus, *pink, white*
I declare against you ...... Liquorice, *purple*
I engage you for next dance Ivy Geranium, *violet*
I forgive you .... Balsam, *white*
I feel much obliged .... Flax (Linum), *blue*
I have lost all.............. Sweet Scabious, *dark violet*
I have a message for you.... The Common Iris, *blue*

40

I live only for you.........	A Leaf of Fennel, *green*
I love	Rose or Chrysanthemum, *red*
I prefer you.................	Large Geranium, *pink*
I refuse you.................	Ice Plant, *pale pink*
I shall quarrel..............	Garden Yarrow, *dark pink*
I tremble	Aspen Leaf, *green*
I will think of it	China Aster, *pink or white*
I want kindness.............	Canariensis, *yellow*
I wish to please.............	Mezereon, *red*
I believe you	Potentilla, *scarlet*
I am dazzled by your charms	Ranunculus, *golden*
I am worthy of you	A Full-blown Rose, *white*
If you love me you'll find me	A Maiden's Blush Rosebud, *white*
Ill-timed raillery	Wild Sorrel, *green*
Imagination	Angelica, *light green*
Impatience	Balsam, *red*
Industry	Clover, *red*
Indifference	Candytuft, *white*
Indiscretion	A Split Reed, *brown*
Ingenuous simplicity	Mouse Ear, *blue*
Independence	A ripe plum, *purple*
Insinuation.................	Bindweed, *white*
Intoxication	A Bunch of Grapes, *purple*

41

J

Jealous of honour .... Globe Ranunculus, *yellow*

Jealousy .... Hyacinth, *yellow*

Jealous resolves........... Balsam, *yellow*

Joyful life .... Lucerne, *crimson*

Joyful tidings............. Wake Robin, *scarlet*

L

Lady deign to smile .... Oak Geranium, *pink*

Languishment .... Cowslip, *pale yellow*

Large family .... Hen & Chicken Daisy, *red & white*

Largeness .... A Gourd, *green*

Liberty.................. Heath, *white or pink*

Light heartedness.......... The Shamrock, *green*

Live for me.............. Garden Mallow, *pink*

Love secret and sincere .... Honey Flower, *white*

Love at first sight......... Coriopsis, *yellow and brown*

Love with anxiety.......... Columbine, *blue*

M

Majesty .... The Persian Lilac, *lilac*

Malevolence .... Lobelia, *lilac*

Meekness .... Heath Broom, *yellow*

Melancholy.............. Yew, *dark green*

Mental superiority .... Flowering Clematis, *white*

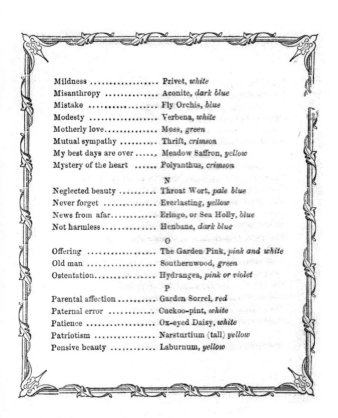

Mildness .... Privet, *white*

Misanthropy .... Aconite, *dark blue*

Mistake .... Fly Orchis, *blue*

Modesty .... Verbena, *white*

Motherly love.............. Moss, *green*

Mutual sympathy .... Thrift, *crimson*

My best days are over ...... Meadow Saffron, *yellow*

Mystery of the heart ...... Polyanthus, *crimson*

N

Neglected beauty .... Throat Wort, *pale blue*

Never forget .... Everlasting, *yellow*

News from afar............ Eringo, or Sea Holly, *blue*

Not harmless.............. Henbane, *dark blue*

O

Offering .... The Garden Pink, *pink and white*

Old man .... Southernwood, *green*

Ostentation................ Hydrangea, *pink or violet*

P

Parental affection .... Garden Sorrel, *red*

Paternal error .... Cuckoo-pint, *white*

Patience .... Ox-eyed Daisy, *white*

Patriotism .... Narsturtium (tall) *yellow*

Pensive beauty .... Laburnum, *yellow*

Perfection .... Pine Apple, *yellow*
Perseverance .... Violet, *purple*
Persuasion .... Garden Mallow, *deep pink*
Pettishness................. Balsam, *variegated*
Pity .... Japonica, *yellow*
Playful mischief .... Hyacinth, *blue*
Pleasure .... Butterfly Orchis, or London Pride
Pleasure of memory........ Periwinkle, *blue*
Plenty .... Corn Flower, *blue*
Poet's glory............... Branch of Bay, *dark green*
Poor but happy............ Vernal Grass, *green*
Poor, yet in hope .... Clematis, *green*
Pride of riches .... Polyanthus, *yellow and brown*
Pride, with jealousy........ Amaryllis (day lily) *yellow*
Profit...................... Cabbage, *green*
Prohibition .... Privet, *white*
Promptitude .... Ten-week Stock, *red*
Prosperity .... Fir Tree, *green*
Protect me .... Bindweed, *white*
Purity .... Hyssop, *white*
Purity and sweetness ...... Jerusalem Lilies, *white*

R

Recantation .... The Lotus Leaf, *green*

Reconciliation .... Filbert Nut, *brown*

Refinement .... Clarkia Pulchella

Remember Early Friendship Periwinkle, *red or white*

Remembrance .... Rosemary, *green*

Remorse .... Raspberry, *red*

Resolved to win............ Columbine, *purple*

Respect and Love .... Sweet Pea, *pink*

Respect and Friendship .... Sweet Pea, *white*

Resistance .... Tansy, *yellow*

Restoration................ Oriental Persicaria, *crimson*

Retaliation .... Scotch Thistle, *purple*

Retirement .... Hare-bell, *blue*

Return of happiness........ Lilies of the Valley, *white*

Reward of merit............ Wreath of Bay, *dark green*

Rudeness.................. Xanthium, *yellow*

Rural joy.................. Grape Vine, *purple*

S

Safety .... Traveller's Joy, *white*

Sans souci (without care) .. Marigold, *golden yellow*

Scandal................... Cobœa, *blue*

Secret .... Maiden-hair, *white*

Sensibility .... Sensitive Plant, *pale yellow*

Sickness .... Anemone, *pale pink*

Sighs...................... Evening Primrose, *yellow*
Sincerity .... Honesty, *pink*
Sincere & unpresuming love Nemophilla, *cerulean blue*
Single .... Maid-wort, *white*
Single from choice .... Bachelor's Buttons, with Leaves
Single from necessity ..... Bachelor's Buttons without Leaves
Single from choice (Ladies) Fair Maid of France, with Leaves
Single from necessity(Ladies) Fair Maid of France, without ditto
Slander.................... Snake's Tongue, *olive green*
Sleep...................... Poppy, *white*
Slighted love .... Chrysanthemum, *yellow*
Snare .... Snap Dragon, *various*
Sorrowful remembrance .... Pheasant's Eye, *scarlet*
Splendour .... Narsturtium, *scarlet*
Strength of mind .... Fennel, *yellow*
Succour .... Balsam, *green*
Success attend you .... Coronella, *pink*
Successful love .... Damask Rose, *red*
Sunshine .... Crocus, *yellow*
Superior merit .... A Moss Rose, *pink*
Support me, or I fall ...... Hawkweed, *yellow*
Suspicion.................. Mushroom, *brownish white*
Sympathy in trouble........ Weeping Willow, *green*

T

Temperance	Azalia, *white*
Temptation	An Apple
Thine for ever	Dahlia, *white*
Token of affection	Daisy, *pink*
Touch me not	Sensitive Plant, *pale yellow*
Trophy of war	Nasturtium Sanguinæ, *dark red*
Truth	St. John's-wort, or Bitter-sweet

U

Unanimity	Phlox, *white*
Unceasing regret	Asphodel, *yellow*
Uncertain	Lupine Mutabilis, *blue and white*
Unfading beauty	Stock, Gilly-flower, *red*
Ungrateful for favours	Crow's-foot, *yellow*
United in peace	York & Lancaster Rose, *white & red*
Unpretending merit	Camellia Japonica, *red*
Unrequited merit	Primrose, *red*
Useless, though pretty	Meadow sweet, *white*

V

Variety	China Aster, *variegated*
Victory	Palm, *dark green*
Virtue	Mint, *green*
Vivacity	Meadow Lychins, *pink*

Warmth of affection ...... Cactus, *brilliant pink*
Want of affection .... Mustard, *yellow*
War .... Yarrow, *yellow*
Welcome .... Marigold, *golden yellow*
Welcome news .... Purple-top Clary, *purple*
Woman's love............. Clove Scented Carnation, *white*
Witchcraft .... Enchanter's Nightshade, *purple*
Wisdom .... Sage, *green*
Wisdom .... A Mulberry, *purple*
Wit .... Ragged Robin, *pink*
Widowhood .... Sweet Scabious, *dark purple*
Welcome to strangers ...... Michaelmas Daisy, *red and yellow*

Y

You admire yourself ...... Narcissus, *white*
You are rich in attraction .. Ranunculus, *scarlet*
You are a coquette .... Queen's Rocket, *white*
You are charming.......... A Musk Rose, *red*
You dot on a fool .... Love in Idleness, *red*
You will cause my death .. Hemlock, *purple*
Youthful days .... Buttercup, *golden yellow*

FINIS.

48

Lightning Source UK Ltd.
Milton Keynes UK
UKHW021146140620
364908UK00006B/982